Alfred's Premier Piano Course

Gayle Kowalchyk • *E. L. Lancaster*

Notespeller 2B is designed to be used with Lesson Book 2B of *Alfred's Premier Piano Course*. It can also serve as an effective supplement for other piano methods.

Notespeller 2B reinforces note-reading concepts presented in the Lesson Book through written exercises. Note and interval identification exercises are presented to provide systematic reinforcement to help the student read and write notes on the staff.

The pages in this book correlate page by page with the materials in Lesson 2B. They should be assigned according to the instructions in the upper right corner of pages in this book. They also may be assigned as review material at any time after the student has passed the designated Lesson Book page.

Look for QR codes (▦) throughout the book.

1. Download a free QR code app to a smart phone from iTunes® or Google Play™.
2. Open the app, and then hold the smart phone above the QR code.

Within seconds, a Premier Online Assistant video corresponding to the page in this book will play. These videos provide additional explanations of concepts.

In addition to written exercises, unique features of the book include:

- Short explanations of musical concepts to use as a review before completing the written activities.
- Reinforcement of the rhythm patterns introduced in Lesson 2B.
- Note-reading exercises that introduce the student to famous composers.
- Colorful illustrations that relate to the art used in Lesson 2B.

Illustrations by Jimmy Holder

Copyright © 2014 by Alfred Music
All Rights Reserved. Printed in USA.

ISBN-10: 1-4706-1490-1
ISBN-13: 978-1-4706-1490-4

5-Finger Pattern and Chord Review

1. Name each note in the major 5-finger patterns.
   Then, play and count aloud.

A Major

a.

D Major

b.

G Major

c.

C Major

d.

2. Name the notes in each chord. Then, circle **I** or **V⁷**.

C Major

a.

(Circle one.)

b.

(Circle one.)

G Major

c.

(Circle one.)

d.

(Circle one.)

D Major

e.

(Circle one.)

f.

(Circle one.)

Interval and Term Review

1. Draw lines to connect the intervals to the matching note names.
Then, write the interval name (2nd, 3rd, 4th, 5th, 6th) on the line.

2. Name the notes to fill in the missing letters for the tempo terms.
Then, draw a line from each term to its matching definition.

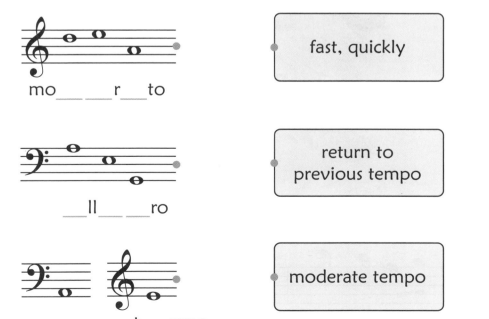

mo___r___to

___ll___ro

___ t___mpo

fast, quickly

return to previous tempo

moderate tempo

4

New Note E in the Bass Clef

1. Draw a half note a 2nd *up* from D. Then, draw a half note a 3rd *up* from Middle C. Name each note.

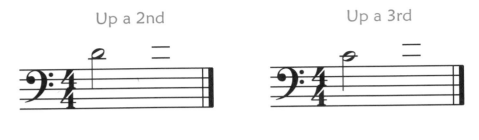

Up a 2nd   Up a 3rd

2. Circle each E on the staff.

3. Draw a line to connect each note to its matching name on one of the boats.

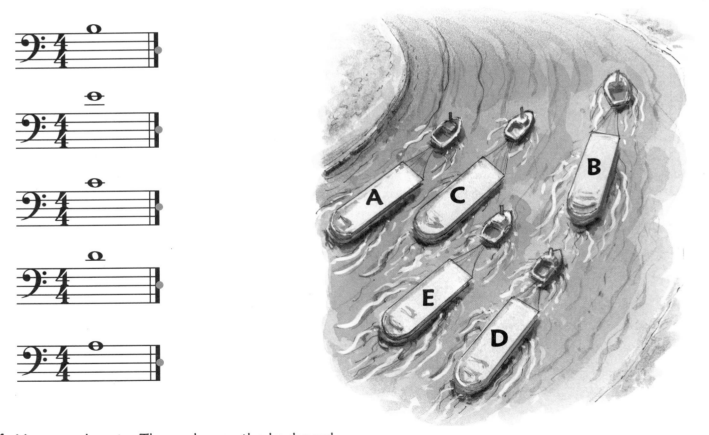

4. Name each note. Then, play on the keyboard.

More About E

1. Using half notes, draw each E three times.

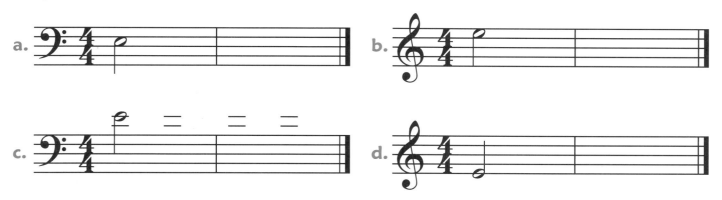

2. Circle each E on the grand staff.

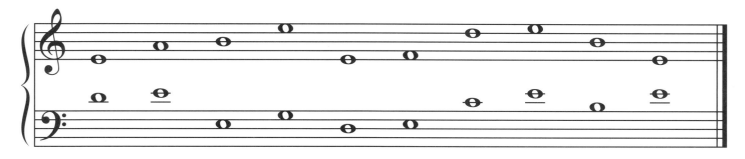

3. Name each note. Then, play on the keyboard.

4. Name the notes to fill in the missing letters for this tempo term.

__n____nt__ = w__lkin__ t__mpo

Lesson Book: pages 8–9

New Notes A and B in Treble Clef

1. Draw a half note a 2nd *down* from Middle C. Then, draw a half note a 3rd *down* from Middle C. Name each note.

Down a 2nd   Down a 3rd

2. Circle each B on the staff.

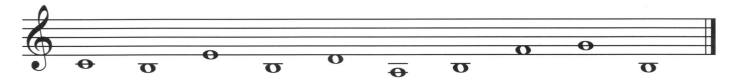

3. Circle each A on the staff.

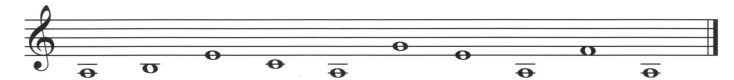

4. Name each note. Then, play on the keyboard.

5. Draw a line to connect each note to its matching name on the banner.

A and D Minor 5-Finger Patterns

1. Name each note in the ascending and descending A minor 5-finger patterns.

2. Name each note in the descending and ascending A minor broken chords.

3. Name each note in the ascending and descending D minor 5-finger patterns.

4. Name each note in the ascending and descending D minor broken chords.

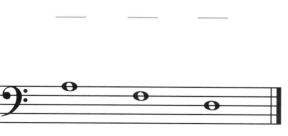

C and G Minor 5-Finger Patterns

1. Name each note in the descending and ascending C minor 5-finger patterns.

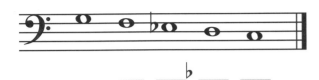 

2. Name each note in the descending and ascending C minor broken chords.

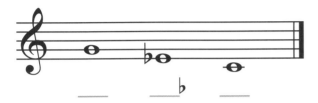

3. Name each note in the ascending and descending G minor 5-finger patterns.

 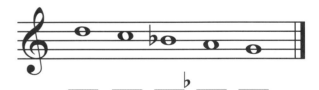

4. Name each note in the ascending and descending G minor broken chords.

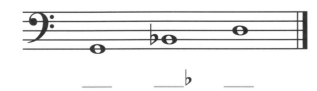 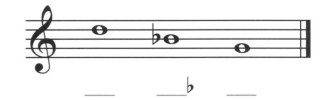

Major and Minor 5-Finger Patterns and Chords

1. Draw lines to connect the 5-finger patterns to the matching note names on a drum.

2. Name each note of the chords.

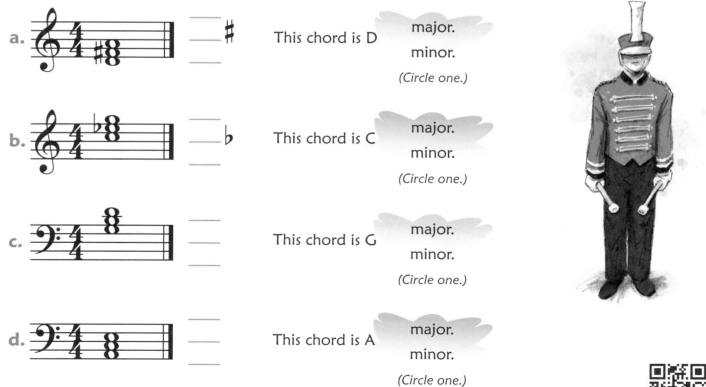

a. This chord is D major. / minor. *(Circle one.)*

b. This chord is C major. / minor. *(Circle one.)*

c. This chord is G major. / minor. *(Circle one.)*

d. This chord is A major. / minor. *(Circle one.)*

Lesson Book: page 14

Hand-over-Hand Arpeggios

1. Name the notes to fill in the missing letters for this term from the music dictionary.

___rp___ ___ ___io   =   ___rok___n   ___hor___

2. Name the notes in each arpeggio. Then, play on the keyboard.

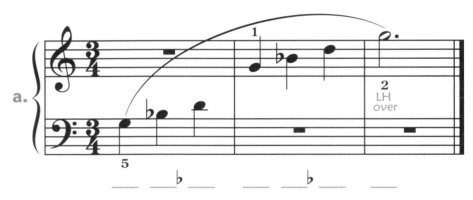

a.

This arpeggio is G   major.

minor.

(Circle one.)

___ ___ ♭ ___ ___ ___ ♭ ___ ___

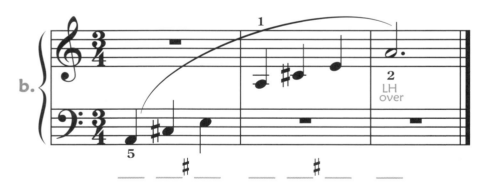

b.

This arpeggio is A   major.

minor.

(Circle one.)

___ ___ ♯ ___ ___ ___ ♯ ___ ___

c.

This arpeggio is C   major.

minor.

(Circle one.)

___ ___ ♭ ___ ___ ___ ♭ ___ ___

More About Arpeggios

1. Draw a line to connect each broken chord in bass clef to the matching broken chord in treble clef.

2. Each of the above broken chords are   major.

                                    minor.

                          (Circle one.)

3. Name the notes in each arpeggio. Then, play on the keyboard.

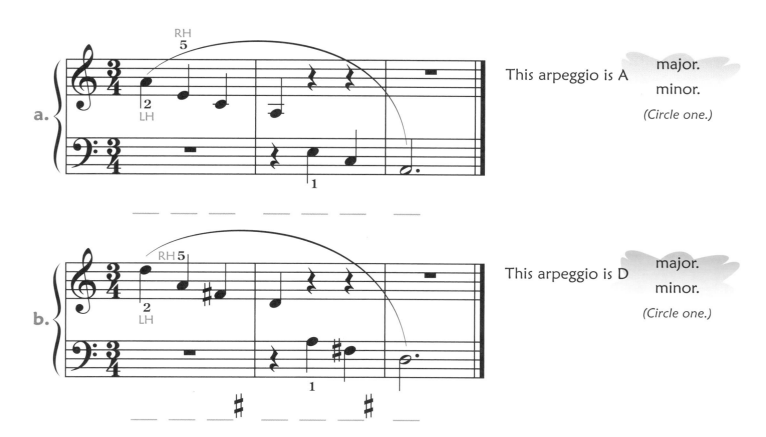

This arpeggio is A   major.

                     minor.

         (Circle one.)

This arpeggio is D   major.

                     minor.

         (Circle one.)

Lesson Book: pages 16–17

Review

1. Draw a line to connect each note to the matching note name on one of the parrots.

2. Name each note of the melodic intervals.

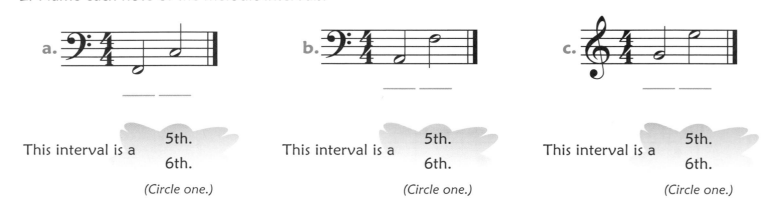

a. _____ _____

This interval is a   5th.
                     6th.

(Circle one.)

b. _____ _____

This interval is a   5th.
                     6th.

(Circle one.)

c. _____ _____

This interval is a   5th.
                     6th.

(Circle one.)

3. Name the notes in the arpeggio. Then, play on the keyboard.

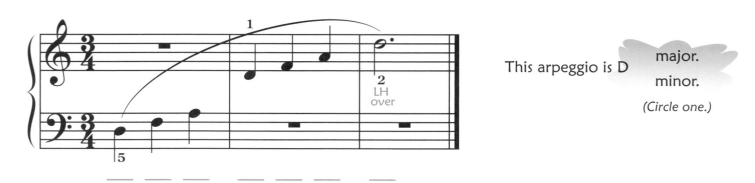

This arpeggio is D   major.
                     minor.

(Circle one.)

_____ _____ _____ _____

Interval of a 7th

On the staff, the notes of a 7th
move up or down:

- from a space to a space,
  skipping three lines and two spaces
- from a line to a line,
  skipping three spaces and two lines

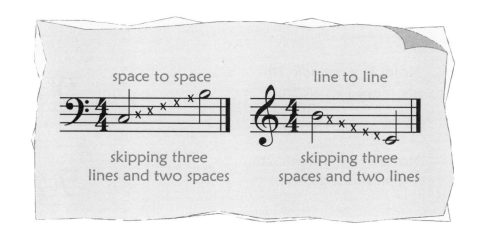

space to space   line to line

skipping three
lines and two spaces

skipping three
spaces and two lines

1. Name each note. Then, cross out the measures that *do not* contain 7ths.

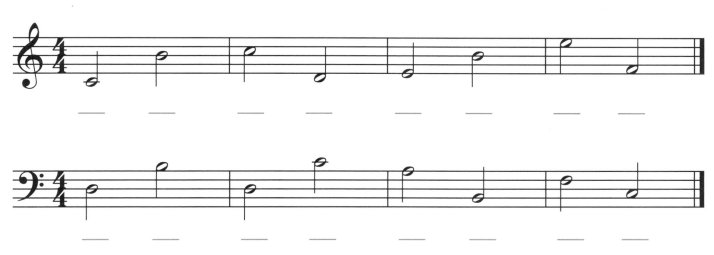

2. Draw a line to connect the 7ths to the matching note names on one of the jerseys.

Melodic and Harmonic 7ths

Notes in a *melodic* 7th
are played *separately*.

Notes in a *harmonic* 7th
are played *together*.

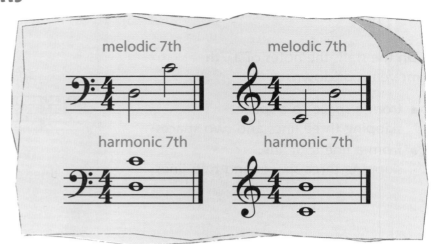

1. Name the notes of each melodic 7th.
   Then, using whole notes, write the notes as a harmonic 7th.

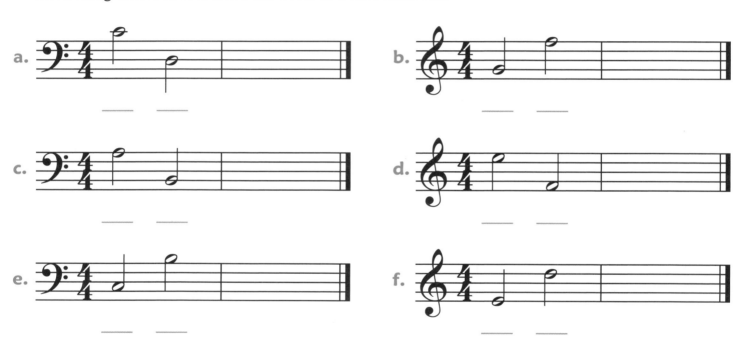

a. _____ _____

b. _____ _____

c. _____ _____

d. _____ _____

e. _____ _____

f. _____ _____

2. Name each note. Then, play and count aloud.

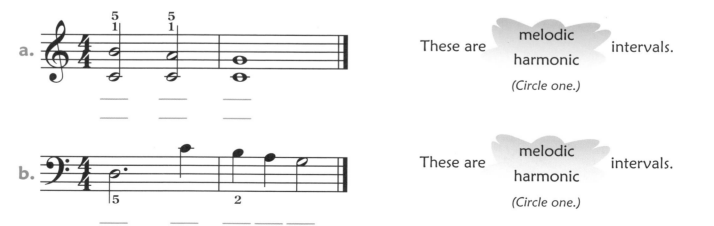

a. _____ _____ _____

These are melodic / harmonic intervals.
(Circle one.)

b. _____ _____ _____

These are melodic / harmonic intervals.
(Circle one.)

Review

1. Name each note of the harmonic intervals.

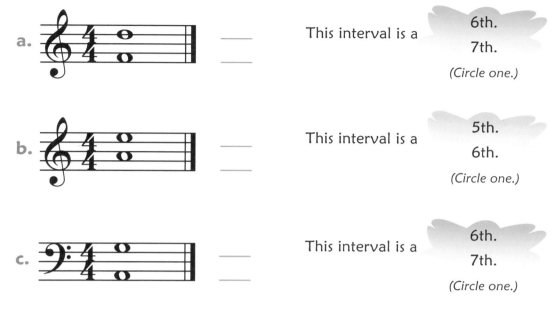

a. _____ _____   This interval is a   6th. / 7th. *(Circle one.)*

b. _____ _____   This interval is a   5th. / 6th. *(Circle one.)*

c. _____ _____   This interval is a   6th. / 7th. *(Circle one.)*

d. _____ _____   This interval is a   4th. / 5th. *(Circle one.)*

2. Name the notes to learn about this famous composer.

Meet Johannes Brahms (1833–1897)

Joh___nn___s ___r___hms w___s ___ ___ ___rm___n

___ompos___r. His ___ ___st ___ri___n___ w___s ___l___r___

S___hum___nn. Sh___ inspir___ ___ ___ m___ny o___ his ___ompositions.

H___ is most ___ ___ ___mous ___or his symphoni___s ___n___ pi___no musi___.

Legato Pedaling

Lesson Book: page 22

Name the notes to learn about legato pedaling.

1. Th___ ___mp__r p___l is pr__ss__ __own.

2. Th___ ___lt __ __mp__rs li__t o___

   th ___ strin___s.

3. Soun___ ___ontinu__s __ __t__r th___ k___ys

   __r___ r__l__s___.

4. L___to p___ __lin___

   __r__t__s smooth, l___to soun___s.

5. ___s you p___l, k___p your h___l on th___ ___loor.

Interval of an Octave (8th)

On the staff, the notes of an
octave (8th) move up or down:

- from a space to a line,
  skipping three lines and three spaces
- from a line to a space,
  skipping three spaces and three lines

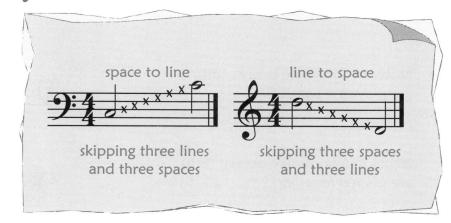

space to line

skipping three lines
and three spaces

line to space

skipping three spaces
and three lines

1. Name each note. Then, cross out the measures that *do not* contain octaves (8ths).

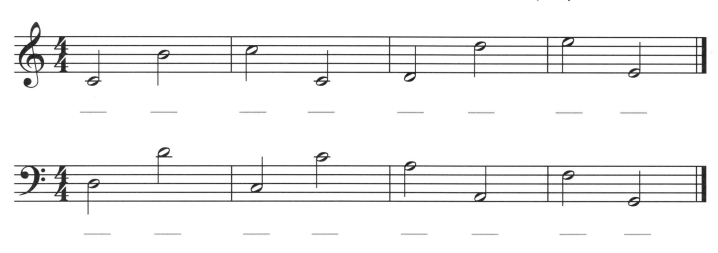

2. Draw a line to connect the octaves to the matching note names.

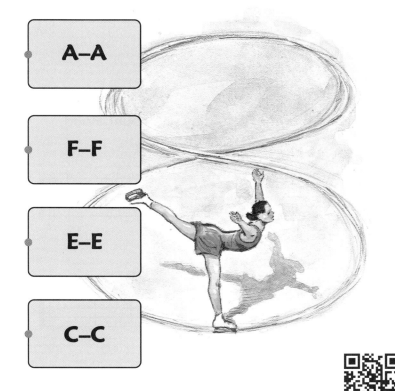

A–A

F–F

E–E

C–C

Lesson Book: page 25

Melodic and Harmonic Octaves (8ths)

Notes in a *melodic* octave (8th)
are played *separately*.

Notes in a *harmonic* octave (8th)
are played *together*.

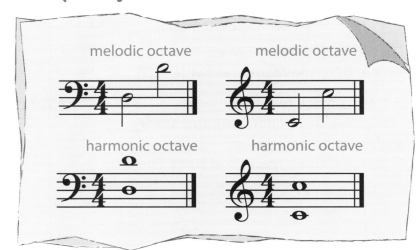

1. Name the notes of each melodic octave (8th).
   Then, using whole notes, write the notes as a harmonic octave.

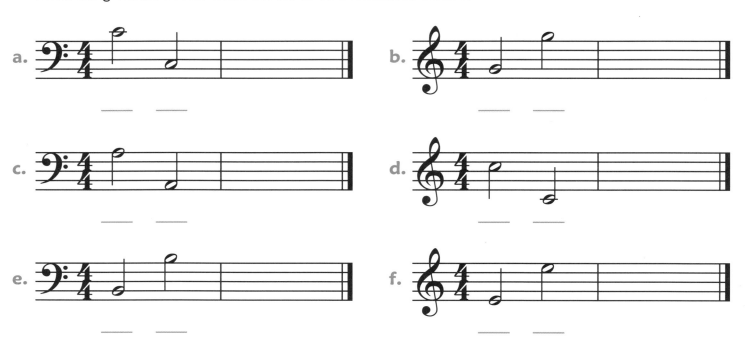

a. _____ _____

b. _____ _____

c. _____ _____

d. _____ _____

e. _____ _____

f. _____ _____

2. Name each note. Then, play and count aloud.

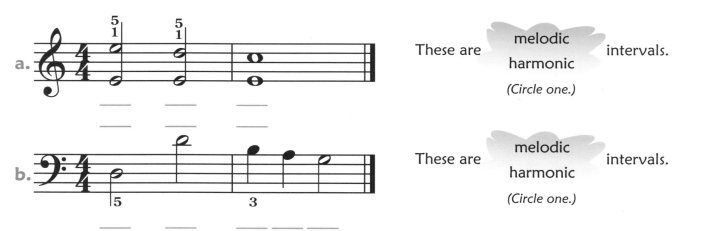

a. _____ _____ _____

These are melodic / harmonic intervals.
(Circle one.)

b. _____ _____ _____

These are melodic / harmonic intervals.
(Circle one.)

Review

1. Name each note of the harmonic intervals.

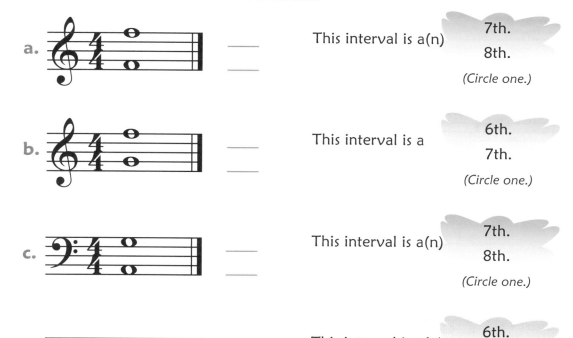

a. _____ _____   This interval is a(n)   7th.
                                          8th.
                 (Circle one.)

b. _____ _____   This interval is a   6th.
                                          7th.
                 (Circle one.)

c. _____ _____   This interval is a(n)   7th.
                                          8th.
                 (Circle one.)

d. _____ _____   This interval is a(n)   6th.
                                          8th.
                 (Circle one.)

2. Name the notes to learn about this famous composer.

Meet Igor Stravinsky (1882–1971)

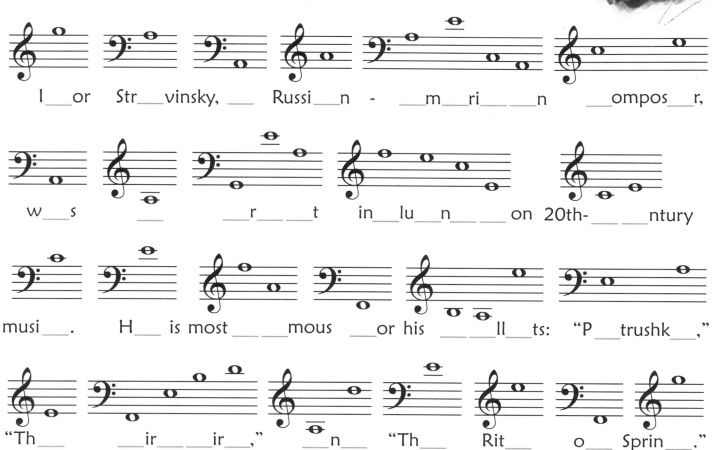

I__or Str__vinsky, __ Russi__n - __m__ri__n __ompos__r,

w__s __r__t in__lu__n__ on 20th-__ntury

musi__.   H__ is most ____mous __or his __ll__ts: "P__trushk__,"

"Th__ __ir__ir__," __n__ "Th__ Rit__ o__ Sprin__."

Lesson Book: pages 28–29

Five Cs

Memorize these Cs as guides to learning other notes.

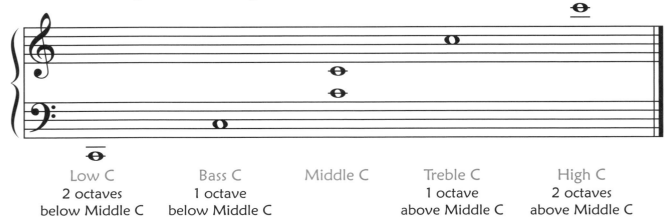

Low C	Bass C	Middle C	Treble C	High C
2 octaves below Middle C	1 octave below Middle C		1 octave above Middle C	2 octaves above Middle C

1. Circle each C on the grand staff.

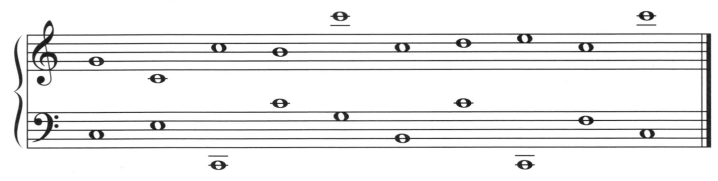

2. Draw a line to connect each note to its matching name near one of the instruments.

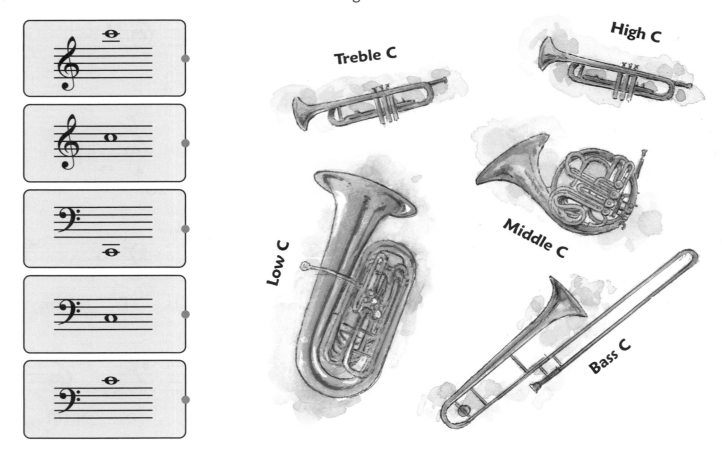

C Major Scale

1. Name each note in the ascending and descending C major scales. Then, play and count aloud.

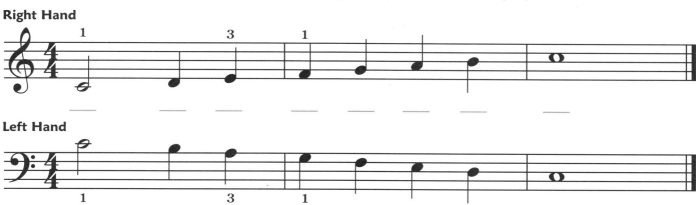

2. Draw a line to connect each interval to the matching note names on one of the shoe boxes. Then, write the interval name (2nd, 3rd, 4th, 5th, 6th, 7th, 8th) on the line.

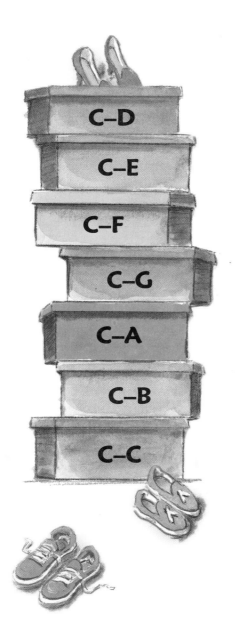

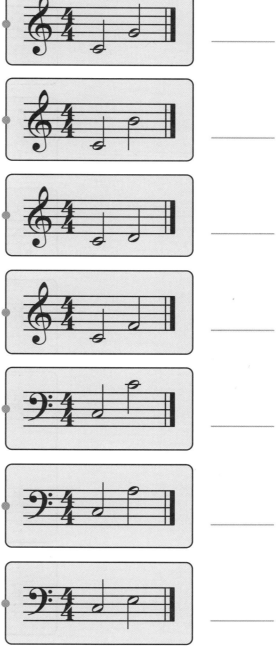

Lesson Book: page 31

G Major Scale

1. Name each note in the descending and ascending G major scales. Then, play and count aloud.

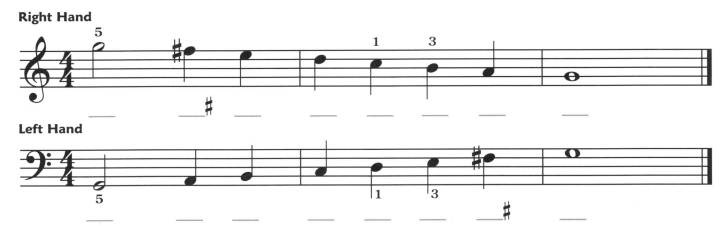

2. Draw a line to connect each interval to the matching note names on one of the baseball gloves. Then, write the interval name (2nd, 3rd, 4th, 5th, 6th, 7th, 8th) in the ball.

Review

1. Name the notes to fill in the missing letters from dynamics in the music dictionary.

a.   pi___nissimo   =   v___ry   so___t

b.   ___ortissimo   =   v___ry   lou___

2. The notes of the C major scale are scrambled below. To build the *descending* scale, begin with treble C and draw a line from one note to the next lower note in the scale.

Begin

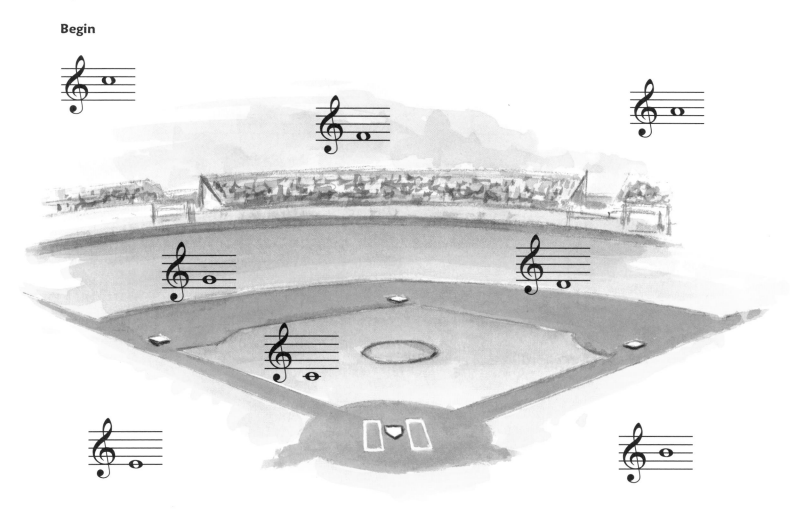

The Three-Note V⁷ Chord in C

The **V⁷** chord is built on the 5th note of the C 5-finger pattern.

It has four notes: G–B–D–F.

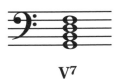

V⁷

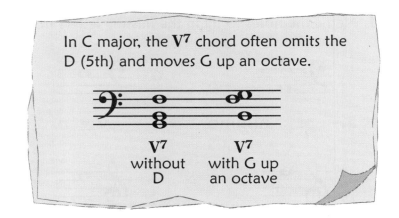

In C major, the **V⁷** chord often omits the D (5th) and moves G up an octave.

V⁷ without D   V⁷ with G up an octave

1. Name each note of the **V⁷** chords in C.

a.   b.   c.

2. Name the notes in the four-note **V⁷** chords in C.

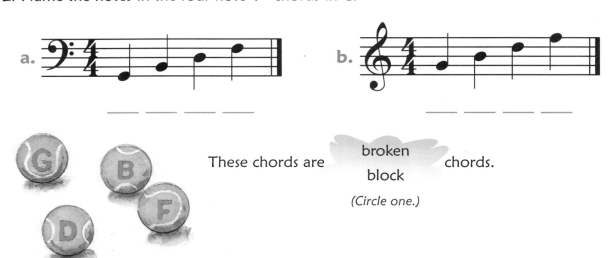

a.   b.

These chords are broken / block chords.
(Circle one.)

V⁷ TENNIS BALLS

3. Name the notes in each chord in C. Then, circle **I** or **V⁷**.

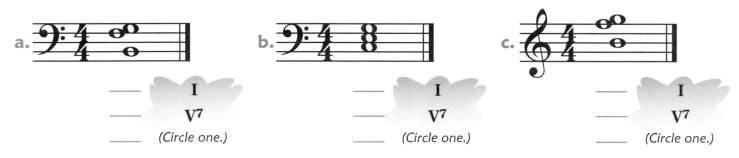

a.   I / V⁷   *(Circle one.)*   b.   I / V⁷   *(Circle one.)*   c.   I / V⁷   *(Circle one.)*

The Three-Note V⁷ Chord in G

The **V⁷** chord is built on the 5th note of the G 5-finger pattern.

It has four notes: D–F♯–A–C.

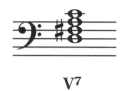

V⁷

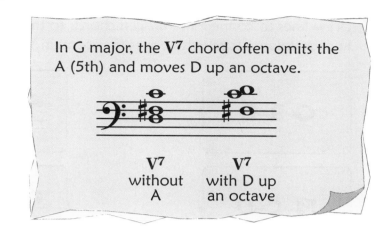

In G major, the **V⁷** chord often omits the A (5th) and moves D up an octave.

V⁷
without
A

V⁷
with D up
an octave

1. Name each note of the **V⁷** chords in G.

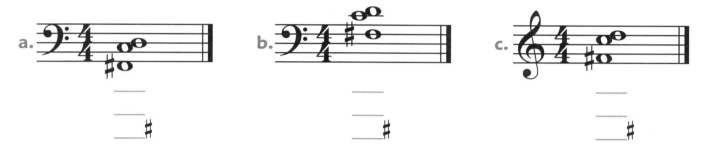

a. ___ ___ ___♯

b. ___ ___ ___♯

c. ___ ___ ___♯

2. Name the notes in the four-note **V⁷** chords in G.

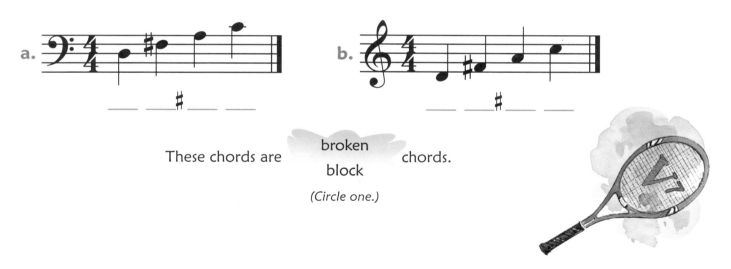

a. ___ ___♯ ___ ___

b. ___ ___ ___♯ ___

These chords are
broken
block
chords.

(Circle one.)

3. Name the notes in each chord in G. Then, circle **I** or **V⁷**.

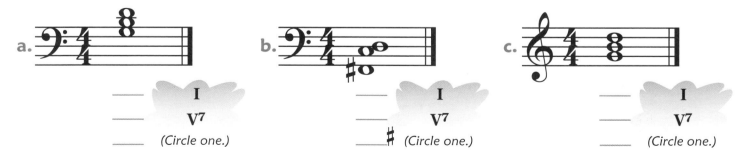

a. ___ ___ ___   **I**   **V⁷**   *(Circle one.)*

b. ___ ___ ___♯   **I**   **V⁷**   *(Circle one.)*

c. ___ ___ ___   **I**   **V⁷**   *(Circle one.)*

Lesson Book: pages 36–37

More About V⁷ Chords and Scales

1. Draw lines to connect the broken chords to the matching note names.
In each column, circle the boxes that contain **V⁷** chords in C or G.

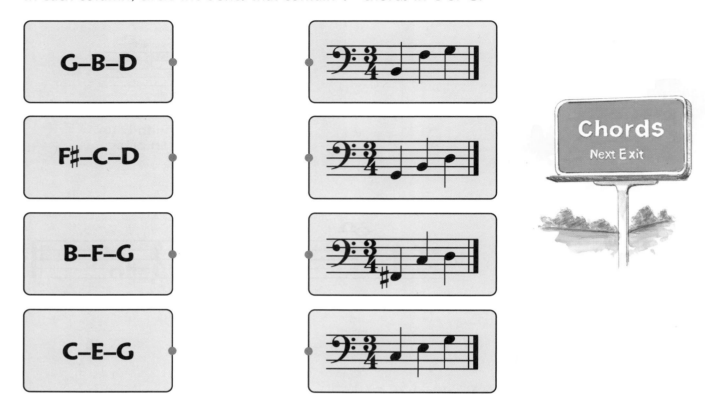

2. The notes of the G major scale are scrambled below. To build the *ascending* scale,
begin with low G and draw a line from one note to the next higher note in the *scale*.

Begin

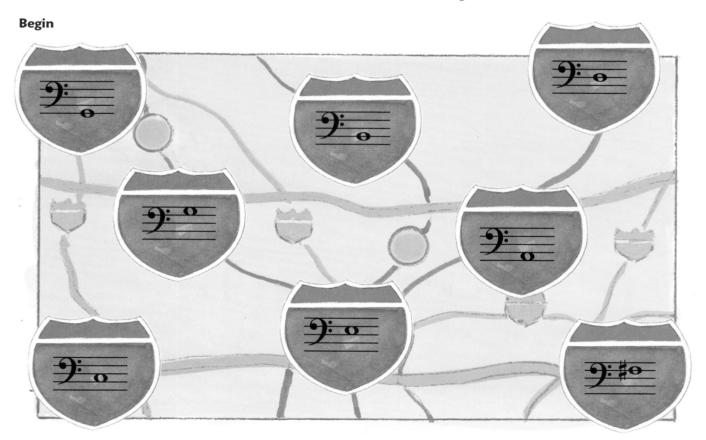

Review

1. Draw a half note to complete each melodic interval. Name the notes.

2. Name the notes to learn about this famous composer.

Meet Robert Schumann (1810–1856)

Ro___rt   S___hum___nn   w___nt___   to

___on___rt   pi___nist,   ___ut his   ___r___m   ___n   ___

wh___n   h___   injur___   his   h___n___.   H___   ___o___us___   on

___omposin___   ___n___   ___   ___m   on___   ___o___   th___

___r___t___st   ___ompos___rs   o___   th___   Rom___nti___   ___r___.

Lesson Book: pages 40–41

Single Eighth Note and Eighth Rest

1. Draw whole notes on the staff to complete the spelling of each rest.

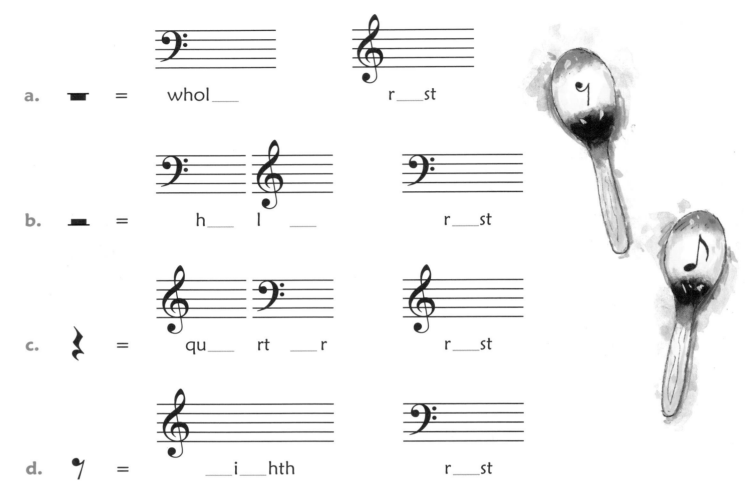

a. ▬ = whol___   r___st

b. ▬ = h___ l ___   r___st

c. 𝄽 = qu___ rt ___r   r___st

d. 𝄾 = ___i___hth   r___st

2. Name each note. Then, play and count aloud.

Dotted Quarter Note

1. Name the notes to fill in the missing letters for the note names and the number of counts they receive.

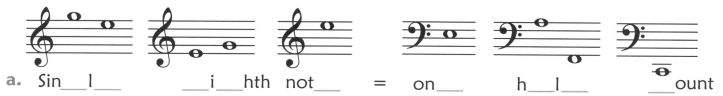

a. Sin__l__ __i__hth not__ = on__ h__l__ __ount

b. Qu__rt__r not__ = on__ __ount

c. __ott____ h__l__ not__ = on__ __n__

on__ h__l__ __ounts

2. Name each note. Then, play and count aloud.

Lesson Book: page 43

Bass Clef Review

1. Name each line note in bass clef.

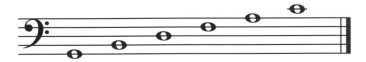

_____ _____ _____ _____ _____

2. Name each space note in bass clef.

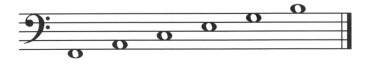

_____ _____ _____ _____ _____

3. Draw a line to connect each interval to the matching note names on the windmill. Then, write the interval name (2nd, 3rd, 4th, 5th, 6th, 7th, 8th) on the line.

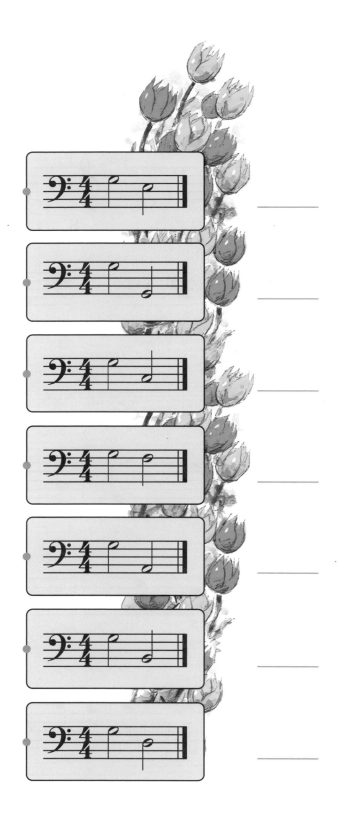

Treble Clef Review

1. Name each line note in treble clef.

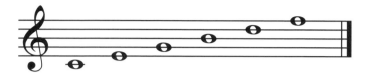

2. Name each space note in treble clef.

3. Draw a line to connect each interval to the matching note names on one of the magnifying glasses. Then, write the interval name (2nd, 3rd, 4th, 5th, 6th, 7th, 8th) on the line.

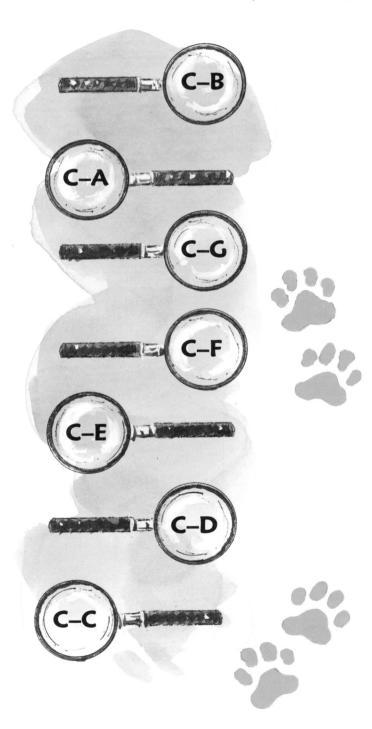

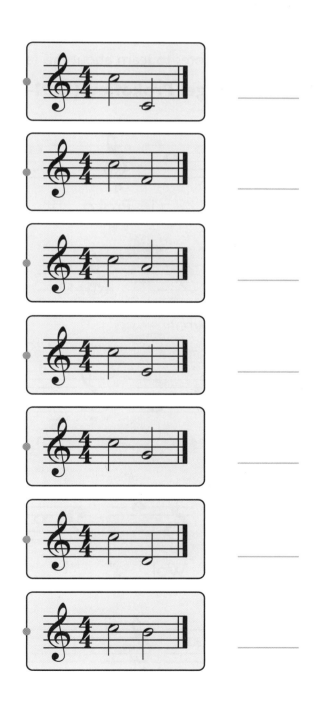

Review

1. Name each note in the ascending C major scale. Then, play and count aloud.

Left Hand

2. Name each note in the ascending G major scale. Then, play and count aloud.

Right Hand

3. Name the notes to learn about this famous composer.

Meet Sergei Prokofiev (1891–1953)

S__r__i Proko__i__v w__s __ Russi__n __ompos__r.

H__ wrot__ __ v__ry __mous pi__ __ __ __or

or__h__str__ __n__ n__rr__tor, "P__t__r __n__

th__ Wol__." H__ is known __or his __on__ __rtos, op__r__s,

symphoni__s, __ilm musi__, __n__ __ll__t s__or__s.